Basic English
for Adult Competency

AUTUMN KELTNER

LEANN HOWARD

FRANCES LEE

Basic English for Adult Competency

Illustrations by MARK NEYNDORFF

Prentice-Hall, Inc., Englewood Cliffs, New Jersey 07632

Library of Congress Cataloging in Publication Data

Keltner, Autumn. (date)
    Basic English for adult competency.

    1. English language--Text-books for foreign students.
I. Howard, Leann.   II. Lee, Frances.
III. Title.
PE1128.K42 1983   428.2′4   82–20555
ISBN   0–13–060418–6

Printed in the United States of America

10   9   8   7

Editorial/production supervision and
        interior design: Barbara Alexander
Cover design: 20/20 Services, Inc.
Manufacturing buyer: Harry P. Baisley

0-13-060418-6

PRENTICE-HALL INTERNATIONAL, INC., *London*
PRENTICE-HALL OF AUSTRALIA PTY. LIMITED, *Sydney*
EDITORA PRENTICE-HALL DO BRASIL, LTDA., *Rio de Janeiro*
PRENTICE-HALL CANADA INC., *Toronto*
PRENTICE-HALL OF INDIA PRIVATE LIMITED, *New Delhi*
PRENTICE-HALL OF JAPAN, INC., *Tokyo*
PRENTICE-HALL OF SOUTHEAST ASIA PTE. LTD., *Singapore*
WHITEHALL BOOKS LIMITED, *Wellington, New Zealand*

Contents

6 Clothing

7 Occupations/Jobs

8 Banking and Postal Services

9 Review

Foreword

Basic English for Adult Competency was developed as a comprehensive guide for teachers whose adult students have had little or no previous exposure to the English language and who may or may not be literate in their native language. The primary purpose of the text is to provide a focus for the development of the functional language skills needed by adults to communicate in situations common in their daily lives.

The overall approach is to introduce simplified, but relevant, communication and to practice generalizations drawn from the language and situations presented. Each page is illustrated with clear visuals which provide a meaningful context for the language being learned. After extensive practice of new patterns through total physical response, drills, and simple dialogues, students are given the opportunity to apply what they have learned through communicative activities such as role play and pair practice. These activities, adapting the language to the students' own real-life situations, are the final and most crucial step in each lesson.

Each lesson follows the same general format:

1. A statement of the competency objective(s) for the lesson
2. Key vocabulary
3. Basic structures
4. Preteaching activities
5. Presentation
6. Supplementary, reinforcement, or review activities

The teacher's edition provides the instructor with step-by-step instructions for presenting the concepts, vocabulary and grammatical structures, and directions for involving students in the meaningful practice necessary for the mastery of the competency objectives. Because of the detailed instructions provided, the text may be used by less experienced teachers, or teachers not accustomed to working with entry level students.

The student should be introduced to the text through the classroom orientation unit included in the teacher's edition. The student text, consisting primarily of visuals, has eight units identical to those in *English for Adult Competency,* Books I and II. The text may be used:

1. independently as an orientation level course,
2. as an introduction to *English for Adult Competency,* Book I and/or,
3. in conjunction with and supplemental to each unit in *English for Adult Competency,* Book I.

Unit nine provides aural comprehension exercises and paired activities designed to review and reinforce mastery of the competencies introduced in the previous eight units. These exercises may also be used as pre-post tests for the competencies.

Priority in sequencing the lessons has been to have each lesson in a unit build on the preceding lessons and to limit the content to that which can be realistically mastered by orientation level students. Every effort has been made to focus the instruction on communication skills which are relevant to the immediate needs of adult refugees and immigrants in their new environment in the United States.

Basic English
for Adult Competency

Identification and Communication

COMPETENCY OBJECTIVES:

On completion of this unit, the students will show orally, in writing, or through demonstration that they are able to use the language needed to function in the following situations:

A. PERSONAL INFORMATION

1. Give upon request self-identification and personal information including name (first, last), address, telephone number, social security number, birthdate, birthplace, age, marital status, and occupation.
2. Fill out simple forms.

B. GREETINGS AND INTRODUCTIONS

1. Make and respond to simple requests for information.
2. Express lack of understanding.
3. Respond to simple questions about the weather.

C. FAMILY RELATIONSHIPS

1. Identify immediate family members.

D. TIME

1. Tell time by the hour and half hour.
2. Identify periods of time in days, months, and years.

E. STATES OF BEING/FEELINGS

1. Express simple states of being and feeling (sleepy, hungry, thirsty, happy, sad, sick).

BASIC STRUCTURES:

Imperative
Be (present)

   Statements and questions
   Affirmative and negative short answers

Be + adjective
Subject pronouns (I, you, he, she, it, they)
Possessive adjectives (my, your, his, her)
"Wh" questions (what, where, how, how old, how many)
Simple present (have)

   Statements and questions
   Affirmative and negative short answers

Her name is Yee Vang.

His name is Tam Lee.

My name is _____.

NAME _____.

NAME

Her first name is Yee.

Her last name is Vang.

My first name is _____.
My last name is _____.

NAME _____
       First   Last

His first name is _____.

His last name is _____.

NAME _____
      First   Last

ADDRESS

Her address is 210 F Street.

His address is _____.

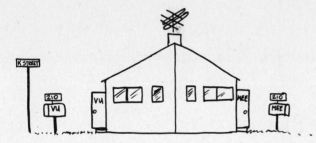

His address is _____.
Her address is _____.

My address is _____.

ADDRESS

His address is 1852 L Street.

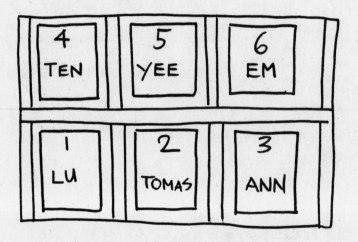

Ann's address is 1852 L Street # _____.

NAME _____

ADDRESS _____

6

NAME   Ann Lee

ADDRESS   1852 L Street #3

CITY   San Diego

STATE

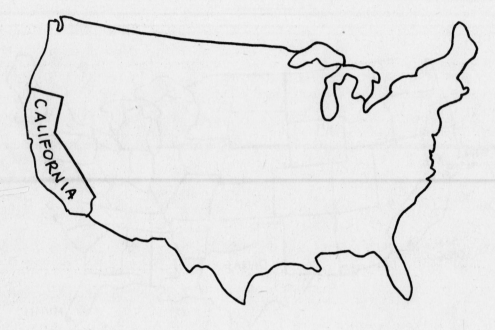

NAME   Ann Lee

ADDRESS   1852 L Street #3

CITY   San Diego

STATE   California

NAME _____

ADDRESS _____

CITY _____

STATE _____

8

ZIP CODE

MIAMI, FLA. 33140

Zip Code _____

WASHINGTON D.C. 20202

Zip Code _____

SAN DIEGO, CA. 92115

Zip Code _____

DALLAS, TEX. 75226

Zip Code _____

NAME _____
      First   Last

ADDRESS _____

_____
    City   State   Zip Code

TELEPHONE NUMBER

My telephone number is _____

TELEPHONE _____

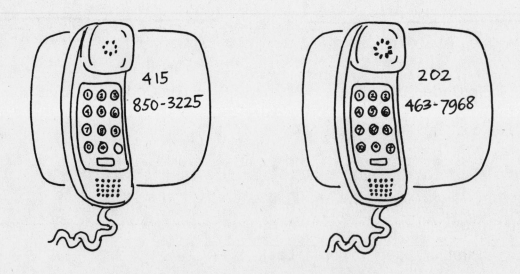

AREA CODE _____ _____

TELEPHONE (_____) _____

PLACE OF BIRTH
COUNTRY OF BIRTH

He is from _____.

His place of birth is _____.

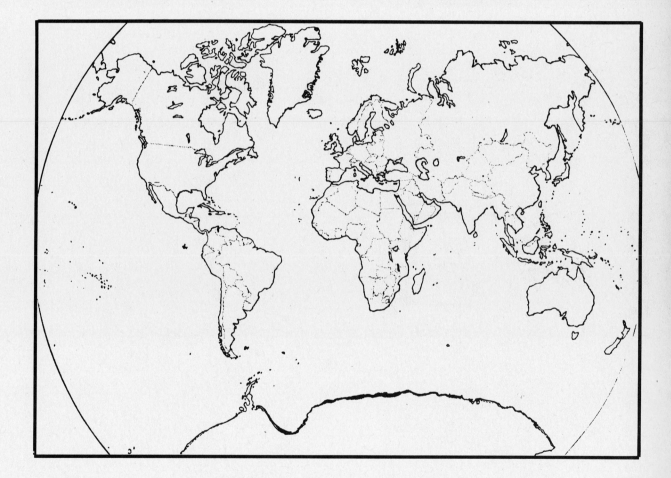

I am from _____.

PLACE OF BIRTH _____.

DATE OF BIRTH
BIRTHDATE

His birthdate is _____.
His date of birth is _____.

Her birthdate is _____.
Her date of birth is _____.

1. His birthdate is May 5, 1945.
    His date of birth is 5/5/45.
    His age is _____.

3. His birthdate is March 4, 1981.
    His date of birth is 3/4/81.
    His age is _____.

2. Her birthdate is June 9, 1948.
    Her date of birth is 6/9/48.
    Her age is _____.

My date of birth is _____.
My birthdate is _____.
My age is _____.

BIRTHDATE _____
DATE OF BIRTH _____
AGE _____

13

FILL OUT THE FORM 1

NAME _____
      LAST   FIRST

ADDRESS_____

_____ (   ) _____
CITY   STATE   ZIP CODE   TELEPHONE

_____
DATE OF BIRTH   PLACE OF BIRTH

PRACTICE

1.	ADDRESS	(213) 473-7095
2.	NAME	May 19, 1946
3.	TELEPHONE	35
4.	BIRTH DATE	Tam Lee
5.	ZIP CODE	210 F Street
6.	AGE	92115

SOCIAL SECURITY NUMBER

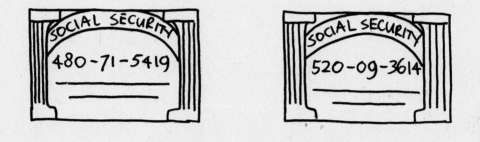

My Social Security number is _____ _____ _____.
SOCIAL SECURITY NO. _____ _____ _____.

FILL OUT THE FORM 2

NAME _____
      LAST   FIRST

ADDRESS_____

_____
CITY   STATE   ZIP CODE   SOCIAL SECURITY NO.

_____
TELEPHONE   BIRTHDATE   PLACE OF BIRTH

PRACTICE

1. NAME
2. ADDRESS
3. TELEPHONE
4. CITY
5. STATE
6. DATE OF BIRTH
7. PLACE OF BIRTH
8. ZIP CODE
9. SOCIAL SECURITY NO.
10. AREA CODE
11. AGE

1. Telephone
2. State
3. Zip Code
4. Place of Birth
5. Name
6. Area Code
7. Social Security No.
8. Address
9. Date of Birth
10. Age
11. City

SINGLE? MARRIED?
MALE? FEMALE?

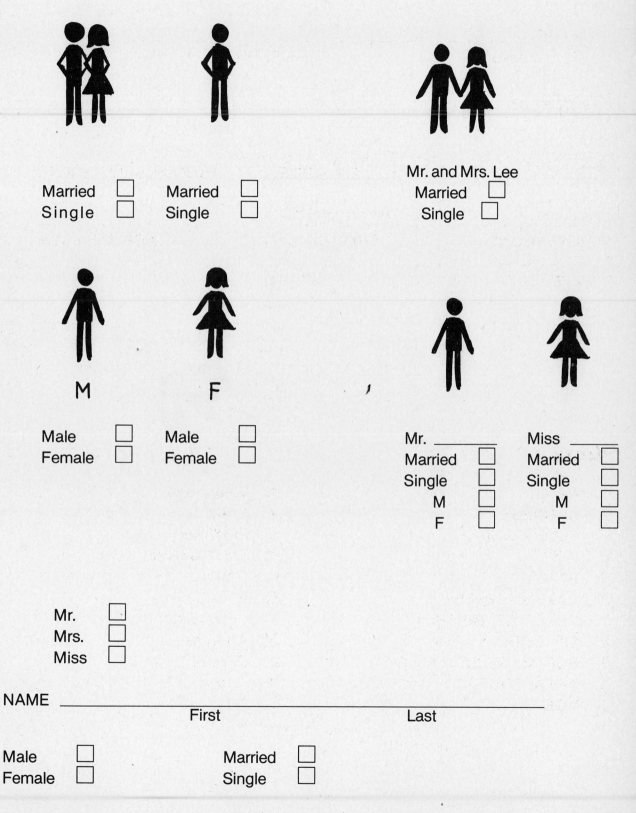

Married ☐
Single ☐

Married ☐
Single ☐

Mr. and Mrs. Lee
Married ☐
Single ☐

M

F

Male ☐
Female ☐

Male ☐
Female ☐

Mr. _____
Married ☐
Single ☐
M ☐
F ☐

Miss _____
Married ☐
Single ☐
M ☐
F ☐

Mr. ☐
Mrs. ☐
Miss ☐

NAME _____
First   Last

Male ☐
Female ☐

Married ☐
Single ☐

FILL OUT THE FORM 3

Mr. ☐
Mrs. ☐
Miss ☐

M ☐
F ☐

NAME _____
          LAST   FIRST

ADDRESS_____

CITY _____ STATE _____ ZIP CODE _____

TELEPHONE _____ SOCIAL SECURITY NO. _____

18

FAMILY

Is he married? _____

How many children does he have? _____

Is she married? _____

How many children does she have? _____

Are you married? _____

How many children do you have? _____

19

THE FAMILY

ID / IDENTIFICATION

1. Please show me your ID.
2. I don't understand.
1. Show me your papers.
2. Oh! Here, they are.

PERSONAL IDENTIFICATION

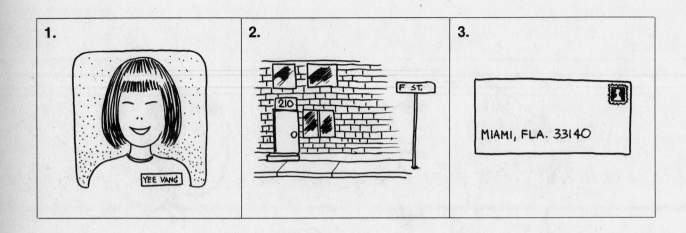

TIME (HOUR)

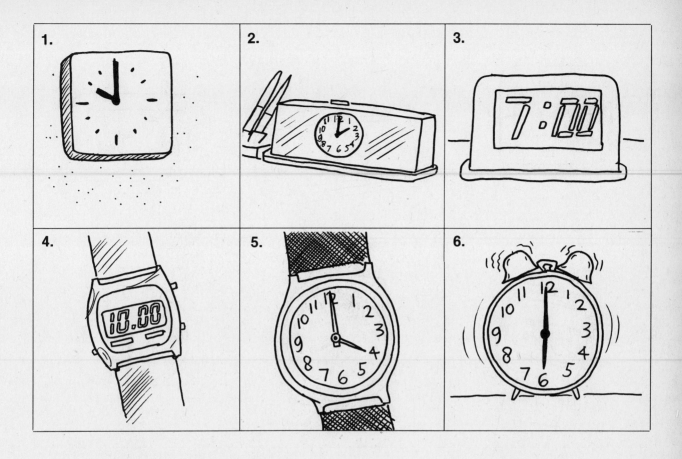

PRACTICE

11:00

3:00

5:00

12:00

WHAT TIME IS IT?

1. **2.** **3.**

4. **5.** **6.**

PRACTICE

3:30

8:30

12:30

6:30

24

IS HE SLEEPY?

HOW'S THE WEATHER TODAY?

SUNDAY	MONDAY	TUESDAY	WEDNESDAY	THURSDAY	FRIDAY	SATURDAY

SUNDAY	MONDAY	TUESDAY	WEDNESDAY	THURSDAY	FRIDAY	SATURDAY

Food and Money 2

COMPETENCY OBJECTIVES:

On completion of this unit, the students will show orally, in writing, or through demonstration that they are able to use the language needed to function in the following situations:

A. SHOPPING FOR FOOD

1. Identify the most common foods.
2. Locate foods in a market.
3. Use simple weights and measures.
4. State food preferences.

B. MONEY

1. Identify and use U.S. coins and currency.
2. Ask the price of an item.
3. Read and calculate simple prices.

BASIC STRUCTURES:

Imperatives
Be (present)
Simple present (like, eat, buy, want, need, weigh)

    Affirmative and negative statements
    Questions

"Wh" questions (where, what, how much, how many)

FRUITS AND VEGETABLES

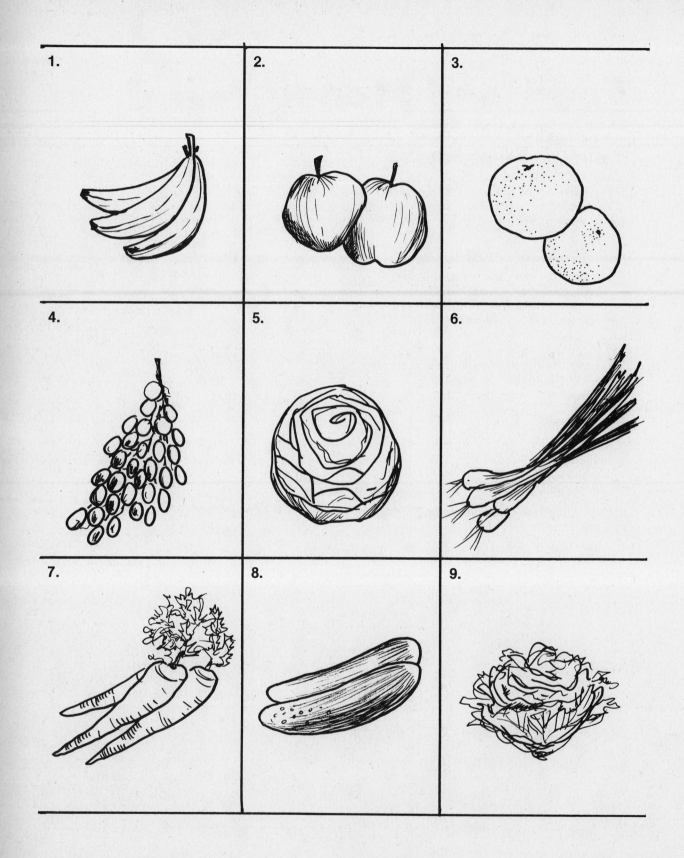

1.

2.

3.

4.

5.

6.

7.

8.

9.

FOODS

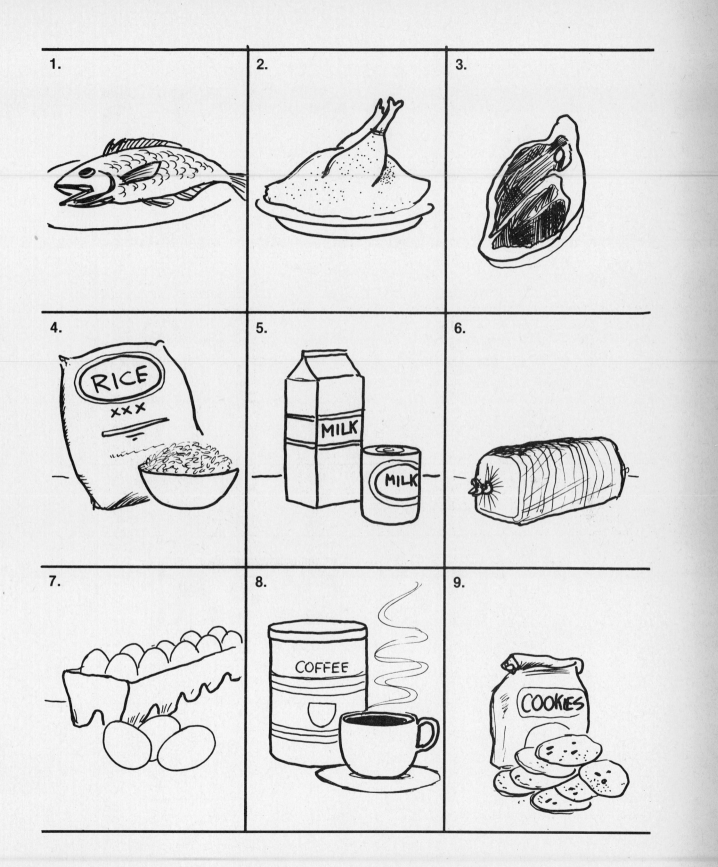

1.

2.

3.

4. RICE xxx

5. MILK / MILK

6.

7.

8. COFFEE

9. COOKIES

MONEY

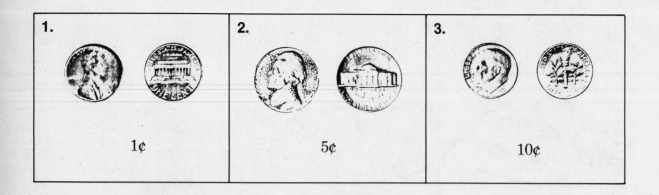

1. 1¢

2. 5¢

3. 10¢

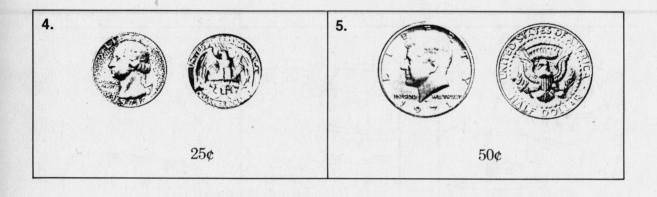

4. 25¢

5. 50¢

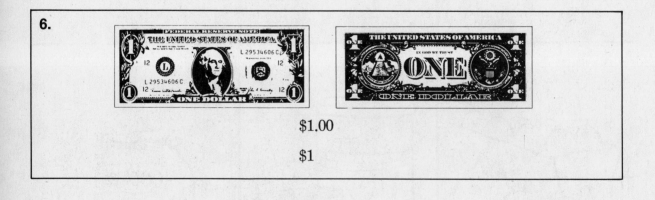

6. $1.00
$1

DOLLARS AND CENTS

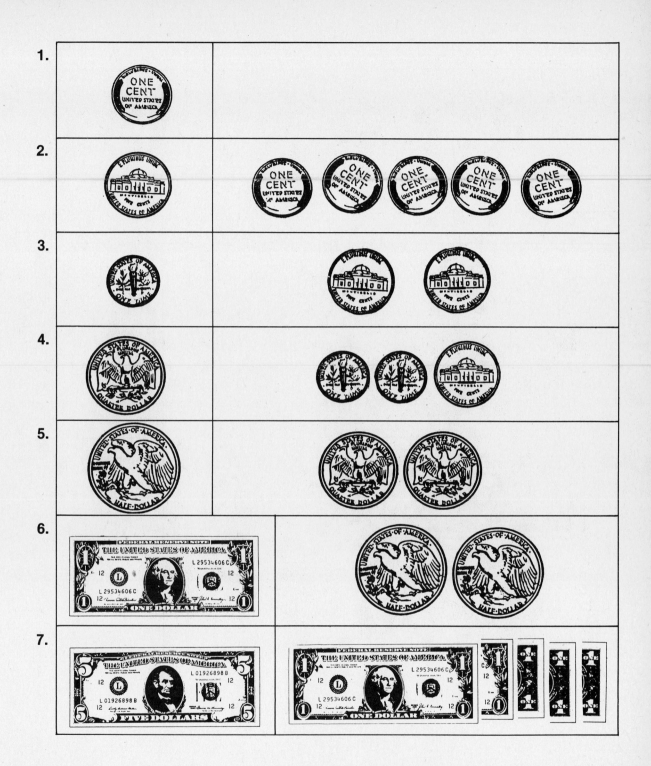

COUNT THE MONEY

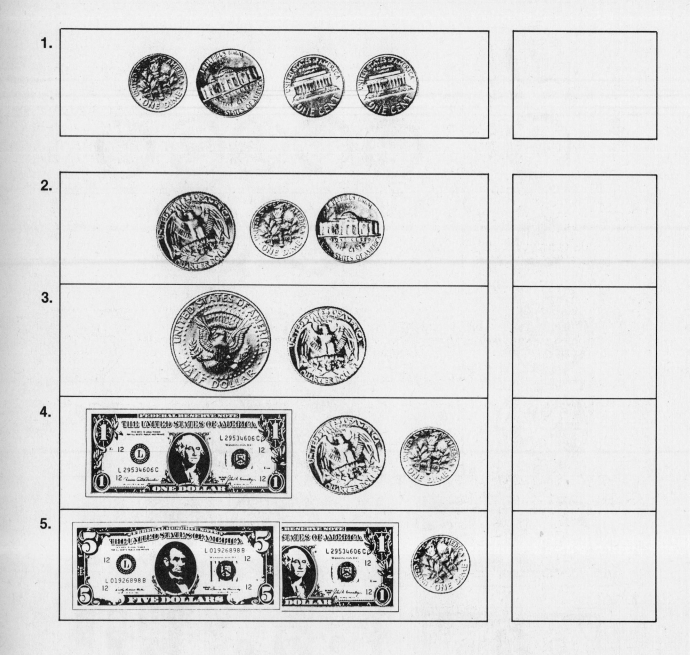

1.

2.

3.

4.

5.

32

HOW MUCH DOES IT WEIGH?

WHAT DO YOU LIKE?

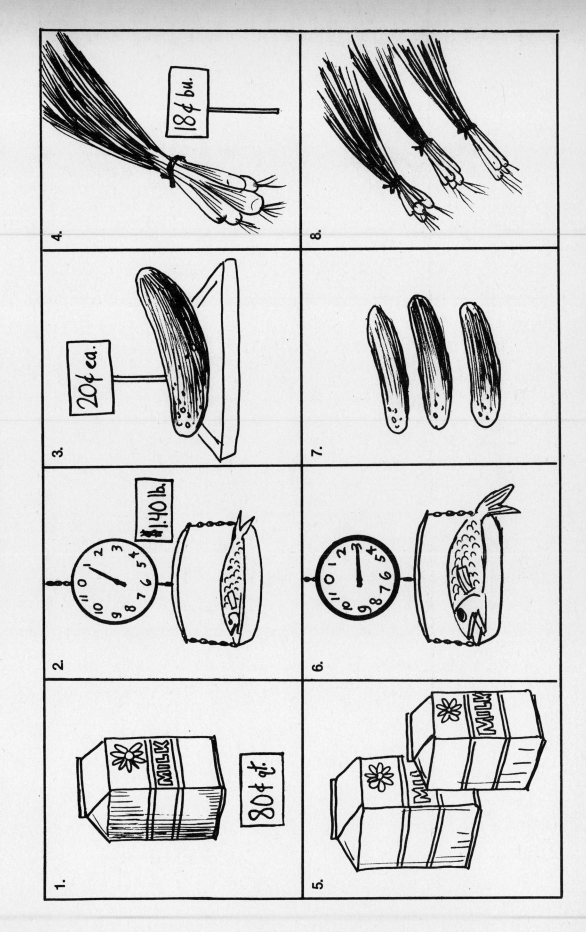

Health and Emergencies

COMPETENCY OBJECTIVES:

On completion of this unit, the students will show orally, in writing, or through demonstration that they are able to use the language needed to function in the following situations:

A. PARTS OF THE BODY

1. Identify and name parts of the body.
2. Describe and respond to questions about common health/dental problems.

B. MEDICAL/DENTAL APPOINTMENTS

1. Tell time in quarter hours.
2. Make an appointment.

C. PRESCRIPTIONS AND DOSAGES

1. Recognize poison labels.
2. Identify common dosages of medication.
3. Follow oral directions for medication.

D. EMERGENCIES

1. Dial "0" for emergencies.
2. Make emergency calls to proper agencies, (police, fire department).
3. Give personal information: name, address, and telephone number.
4. Respond appropriately in event of theft.

BASIC STRUCTURES:

Imperative
Simple present (have, want, need)
Present continuous (call, have, go)
Past (do, steal, take)
"Wh" questions (what, who)
Subject pronouns
Possessive adjectives (my, your, his, her)

THE BODY

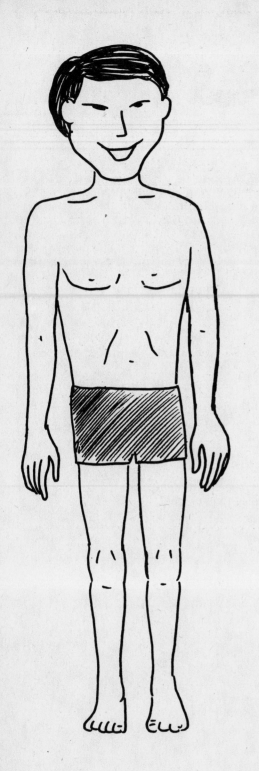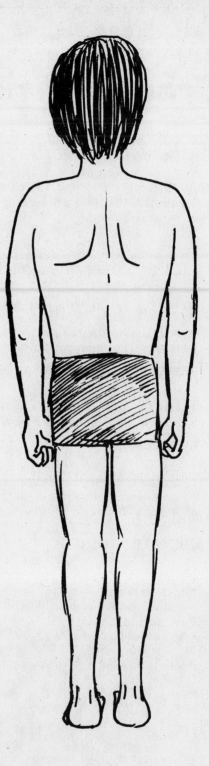

WHAT'S THE MATTER?

MY ARM HURTS

IT'S 8:15

1.

2.

3.

4.

5.

6.

41

IT'S 9:45

1.

2.

3.

4.

5.

6.

42

I WANT TO MAKE AN APPOINTMENT: DOCTOR

AT THE DENTIST

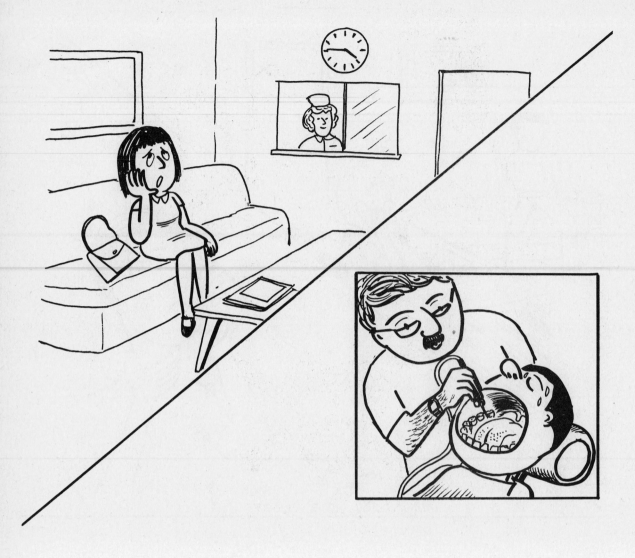

1

Dr. Tom Vu	
NAME:	Kim Lee
DATE:	Monday, May 7
TIME:	10:30 a.m.

2

Dr. John Kelly	
NAME:	Lana Wister
DATE:	Friday, 6–23
TIME:	1:45 p.m.

DON'T DRINK THAT!

POISON   POISON

Keep Out of Reach
of Children

POISON
INFORMATION CENTER
294-6000

TAKE ONE EVERY TWO HOURS

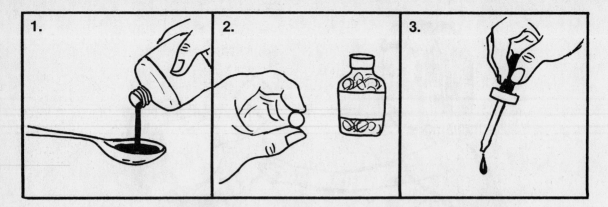

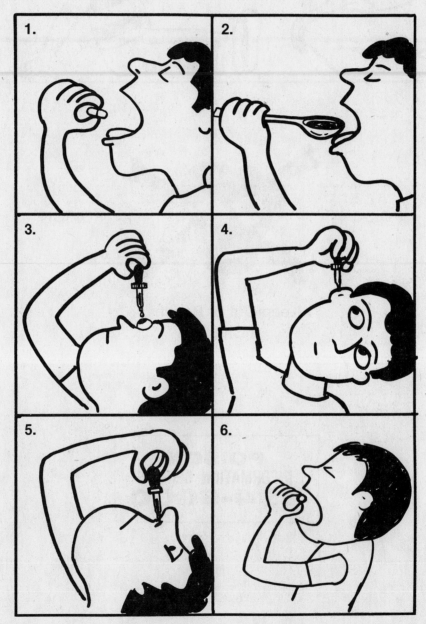

HELP!

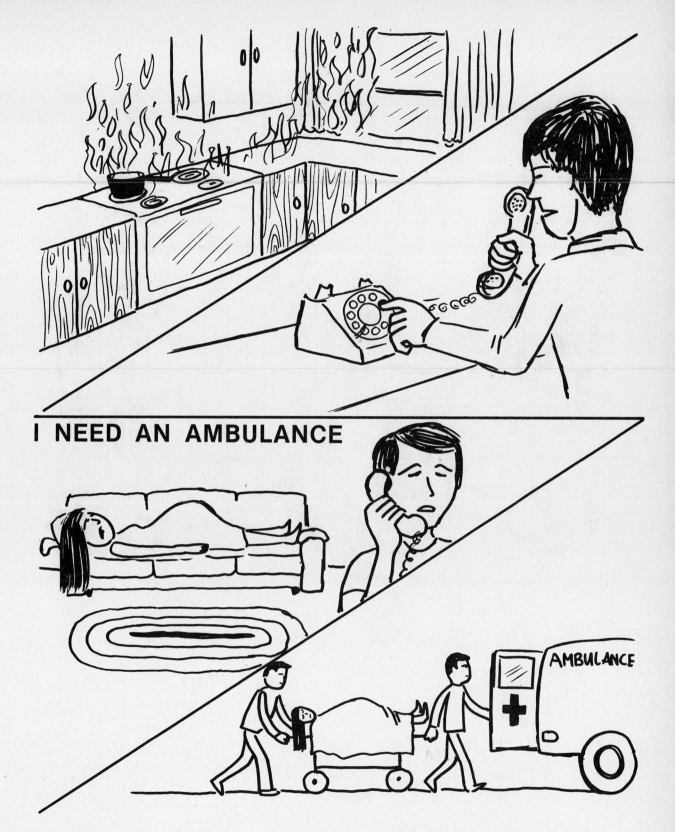

I NEED AN AMBULANCE

GET ME THE POLICE!

Transportation/ Following Directions

COMPETENCY OBJECTIVES:

On completion of this unit, students will be able to show orally, in writing, or through demonstration that they are able to use the language needed to function in the following situations:

A. IDENTIFYING COMMON MEANS OF TRANSPORTATION.

B. FOLLOWING DIRECTIONS.

    1. Simple directions (left, right, up, down).
    2. Finding locations.

C. IDENTIFYING TRAFFIC SAFETY SIGNS.

D. USING A CITY BUS.

BASIC STRUCTURES:

    Simple present (come, walk, go)
    Be (present)
    Past tense, regular and irregular verbs (do, walk, go)
    "Wh" questions (how, when, where, how much, which)
    Imperative, negative
    Prepositions of place

HOW DO YOU COME TO SCHOOL?

PRACTICE

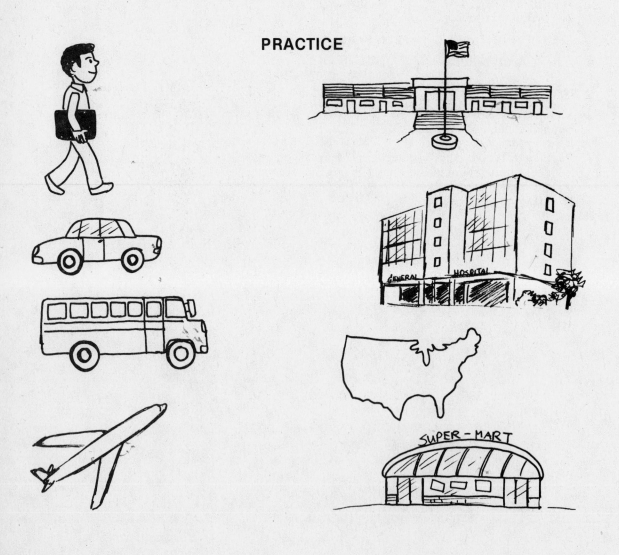

WHERE'S THE OFFICE?

WHERE'S THE BUS STOP?

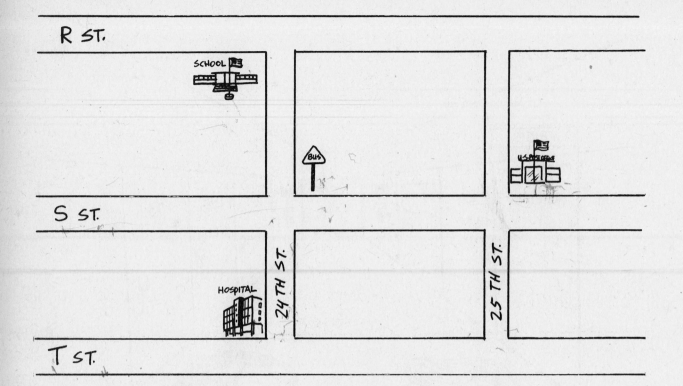

R ST.

SCHOOL

BUS

U.S. POST OFFICE

S ST.

HOSPITAL

24TH ST.

25TH ST.

T ST.

PRACTICE

HOSPITAL

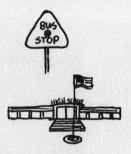

T ST. | 24TH

S ST. | 25TH

24TH
S ST.

24TH
R ST.

WALK / DON'T WALK

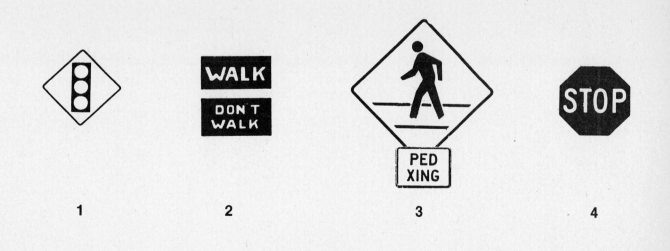

1   2   3   4

HOW MUCH IS THE FARE?

PRACTICE

Housing 5

COMPETENCY OBJECTIVES:

On completion of this unit, the students will show orally, in writing, or through demonstration that they are able to use the language needed to function in the following situations:

A. IDENTIFYING ROOMS AND FURNISHINGS.

1. Name the rooms in a house or an apartment.
2. Identify and locate common household furnishings.
3. Describe common activities at home.

B. IDENTIFYING AND DEMONSTRATING SAFE USE OF APPLIANCES.

1. Demonstrate basic safety measures related to appliances.
2. Respond to request to turn on, turn off, turn up, turn down, plug in, unplug.

BASIC STRUCTURES:

Question with where
Prepositions of place
Present continuous
Imperative

WHERE DOES IT GO?

PRACTICE

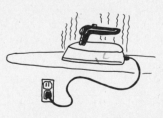

TURN IT ON / TURN IT OFF

WHAT'S WRONG?

Clothing 6

COMPETENCY OBJECTIVES:

On completion of this unit, the students will show orally, in writing, or through demonstration that they are able to use the language needed to function in the following situations.

CLOTHING

1. Identify the most common articles of clothing.
2. Express need or preference for common articles of clothing.
3. Describe clothing in terms of price, color, size, and condition.

BASIC STRUCTURES:

"Wh" questions (what, how much)
Simple present (have, need, want)

   Statements and questions
   Affirmative short answers

Descriptive and demonstrative adjectives

WHAT DO YOU NEED?

YOU

LONG AND SHORT

LARGE AND SMALL

64

OLD AND NEW

PRACTICE

Occupations/Jobs

COMPETENCY OBJECTIVES:

On completion of this unit, the students will show orally, in writing, or through demonstration that they are able to use the language needed to function in the following situations:

A. IDENTIFYING SOME COMMON OCCUPATIONS.

B. STATING THEIR PRESENT AND/OR FORMER OCCUPATIONS.

C. RECOGNIZING SOME BASIC WORK/SAFETY SIGNS.

D. RESPONDING TO SOME WORK-RELATED COMMANDS.

BASIC STRUCTURES:

Imperatives
Be (present and past)

  Statements and questions
  Affirmative and negative short answers.

Present continuous (open, close, push, pull, do, go)

  Statements and questions
  Affirmative and negative short answers

"Wh" questions (what, which)

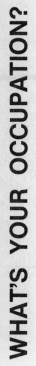

WHAT'S YOUR OCCUPATION?

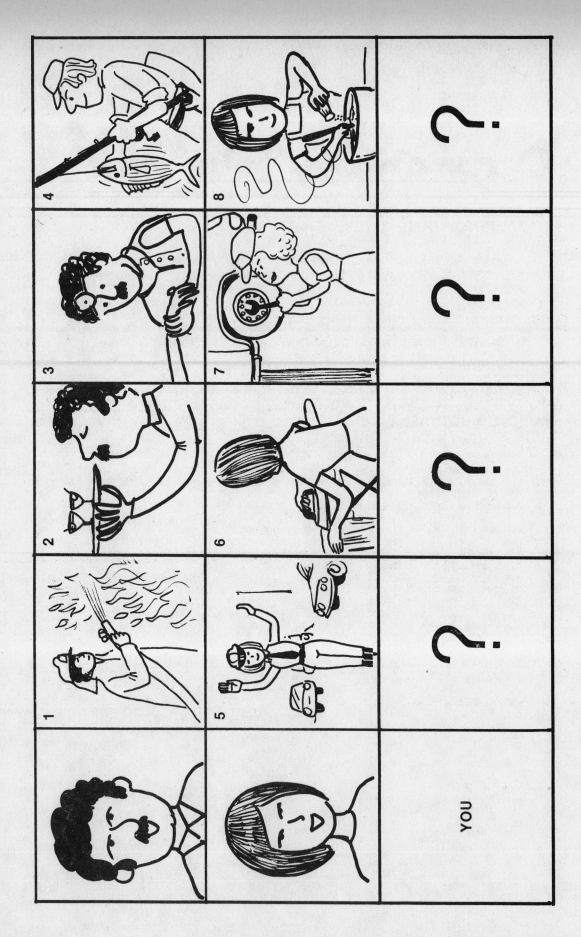

68

WHAT WAS YOUR OCCUPATION?

YOU

?

SIGNS

PUSH / PULL

PRACTICE

1. OPEN
2. IN
3. ENTRANCE
4. UP
5. PUSH

1. EXIT
2. PULL
3. OUT
4. CLOSED
5. DOWN

FIND THE SIGN

PULL

CLOSED

PUSH

DOWN

OPEN

UP

Banking and Postal Services

8

COMPETENCY OBJECTIVES:

On completion of this unit, the students will show orally, in writing, or through demonstration that they are able to use the language needed to function in the following situations:

A. BANK

Deposit or cash a check.

B. POST OFFICE

Ask for money order, postcard, or aerogramme.

BASIC STRUCTURES:

Simple present (sign, want, have, need)
Present continuous (get, give, pay)
"Wh" questions (what, who, how much, where, which)

I WANT TO CASH MY PAYCHECK

PLEASE SIGN

Lee's Department Store   707
851 Roe Street
Longhorn, Texas   January 8 1983

Pay to   Mary Little $72.50

Seventy two and 50/100--- DOLLARS

_____   James Lee

Mary Little

75

AB Cement Company   707
210 Broadway
Pinewood, CA   October 30 19 82

Pay to Cheng Vue $150.00

One hundred fifty and no/100--- DOLLARS

_____   _____ Carlos Medina _____

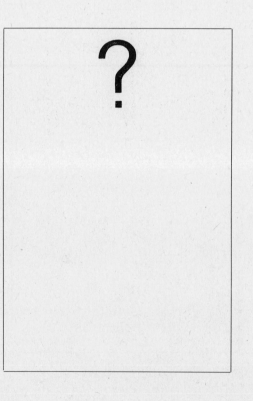

AT THE POST OFFICE

AT THE POST OFFICE

PRACTICE

1. J.Campo
616 Main St.
San Diego
CA 92101

   Mrs. P. Green
   1515 Lake Drive
   St. Paul,

Miss. T. Yang
102 Angel Way
New York, NY 10017

2. Vu Vue
105 Bird St
Orange, Michigan

   Mr. J. King
   3122 - 45th St.
   Los Angeles CA 90004

MN 55102

3. S. Little
14 Olive Lane
Orlando
Florida 32802

4. Greetings from Hawaii

   Jon Lee
   689 Long St
   Pine, OR
   97401

Review 9

COMPETENCY OBJECTIVES:

On completion of this unit, the students will show orally, in writing, or through demonstration that they are able to identify and/or use the vocabulary and structures introduced in the preceding units in functional, communicative activities.

ACTIVITIES

1. Aural Comprehension
2. Pair Practice
3. Dialogues

1.

2.

3.

1.

2.

3.

1.

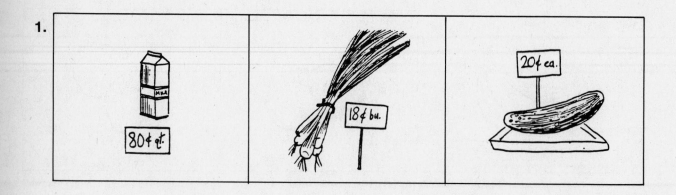

2.

3.

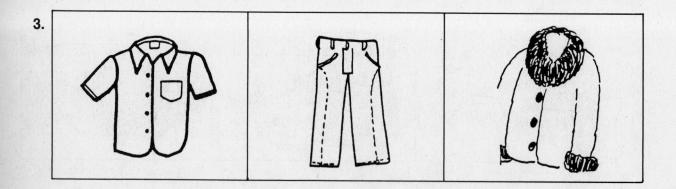

82

1.

2.

3.

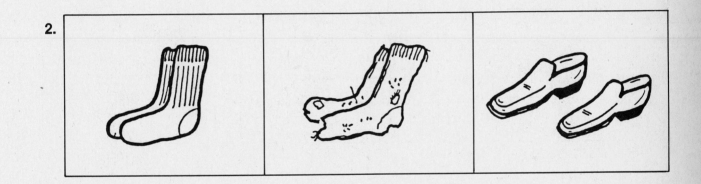

1.

2.

3.

1.

2.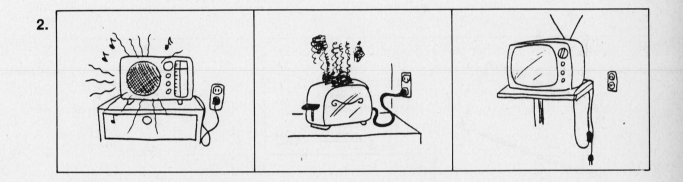

3.

DON'T WALK	WALK	STOP

1.

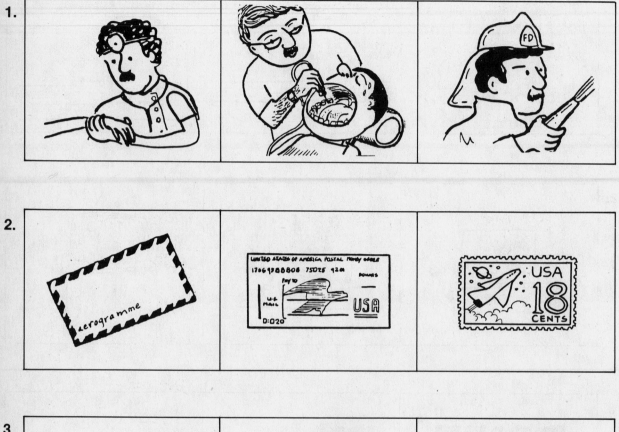

2.

3.

NUMBER REVIEW

1.	210 F Street	290 A Street	710 K Street
2.	33140	92115	75226
3.	464–5173	850–3225	463–7968
4.	714	415	202
5.	1982	1945	1977
6.	560–16–2945	480–71–5419	520–09–3614
7.	4:30	3:15	3:45
8.	17¢	75¢	40¢
9.	$1.35	$6.10	$5.50
10.	80¢ qt.	$1.40 lb.	20¢ each

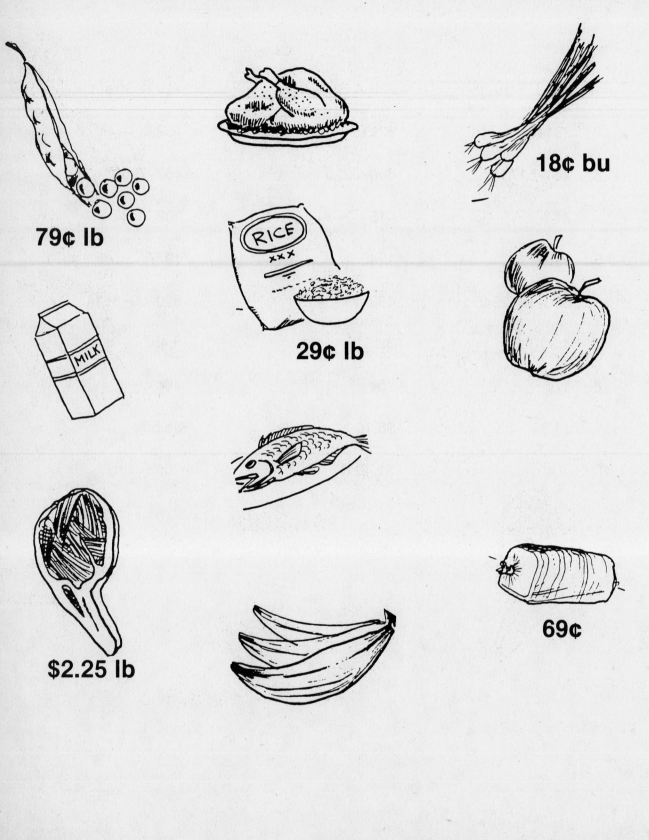

18¢ bu

79¢ lb

29¢ lb

MILK

$2.25 lb

69¢

65¢ lb

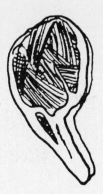

MILK 80¢ qt.

35¢ lb

$1.40 lb

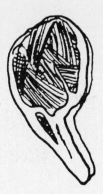

25¢ lb

$35.99

79¢

$7.98

$17.50

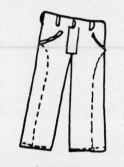

$8.99

$5.95

$6.95

$7.99

TELLING TIME

2:30

7:15

1:00

10:30

4:45

11:15

HOW MUCH DOES HE WEIGH?

WHAT'S THE MATTER?

Ann

Lu

Bob

Ed

Mr. Black

Ask about: Tom, Vu, Mrs. Lee, Joe, Bill

WHAT'S THE MATTER?

Vu

Joe

Bill

Tom

Mrs. Lee

Ask about: Lu, Ed, Bob, Mr. Black, Ann

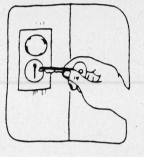

IS THE BANK OPEN?